THE MANY NAMES FOR MOTHER

The Many Names for Mother

Poems by

Julia Kolchinsky Dasbach

The Kent State University Press

Kent, Ohio

Library of Congress Catalog Card Number 2019010988
ISBN 978-1-60635-373-8
Manufactured in the United States of America

The Wick Poetry Series is sponsored by the Stan and Tom Wick Poetry Center and the
Department of English at Kent State University.

LIBRARY OF CONGRESS CATALOGING-IN-PUBLICATION DATA
Names: Dasbach, Julia Kolchinsky, author.
Title: The many names for mother / poems by Julia Kolchinsky Dasbach.
Description: Kent, Ohio : The Kent State University Press, 2019. | Series: Wick poetry
        first book series
Identifiers: LCCN 2019010988 | ISBN 9781606353738 (pbk.)
Classification: LCC PS3604.A824 A6 2019 | DDC 811/.6--dc23
LC record available at https://lccn.loc.gov/2019010988

For the mothers I come from
& the husband and son
who made me a mother

CONTENTS

The Many Names for Mother is a compelling book about origins—of ancestry, memory, and language. Julia Kolchinsky Dasbach's own origins began in 1987 in Ukraine—still a part of the Soviet Union then—and she came to the United States as a Jewish refugee at the age of six. The poems in this collection are peopled by generations of women, brought to life in lucid, moving detail. Here is her mother:

sweating through
tolkuchka—the little push 'n' shove bazar—
to return home with a stained skirt and fruit
dangling from her ears

And here she struggles to encompass all her images of mother:

I've written you as rivers, as frost, as everything
hidden underneath it . . .
. . . as water,
generations and generations of it, mothers'
open hands, as bare Russian birch branches
grasping for clouds, as what a child sees
looking up in a forest.

Many poems are haunted by suffering: war and the holocaust, present-day violence. Dasbach's gift is to bring the past into relevance; we feel its immediacy, almost urgency. In "Letter to My Son" she writes, "Remember, / when half of your ancestors died, the other half / did the killing." Her lyricism can be gorgeous; at times she seems to harness the elements, invoking water, earth, sun, and stars throughout in rich combinations, like bits of genetic code. One in a series of poems entitled "Other women don't tell you" delves into the etymology of the word *mother*, noting the links to "scum and dregs and filth" but also to "cloud."

Dasbach is a searching, patient poet, more interested in questions than answers. What gets passed down through generations? What should be remembered? What forgotten? A particularly heartbreaking set of poems explores how to explain the burdens of history, death, and guns to a son: "*bang, bang,* every night, he sings / all the ways we know how to take." Though Dasbach does not look away from what is painful and disturbing, there are rich images of pleasure as well. She describes food with sensuous simplicity, "lemons / cut to perfect circles and placed / around a gold-rimmed plate / with *pryaniki* and sour cream." She compares the sun to "a Rainier cherry / at its yellow heart, fire / skinned and ripe / with reaching."

This reaching—for meaning, for understanding—is ever present. Dasbach returns again and again to the ongoing struggle between embracing the past and escaping it. She writes:

> The past, a book of mothers
> trying to unlearn how hatred
> festers in the blood
> and passes down.

Another passage speaks of her son's growing body:

> your people's   birth-
> and death-days   frozen in his bones
> though already   the days grow longer now
> by minutes only   like his legs
> more ready to walk away

An insistence on history is at the core of Dasbach's work. I am struck by both its timeliness and timelessness. She explores questions of race and otherness with acute awareness. "Remember, here you are a white man" begins "Letter to My Son." Then later in the poem, "Know, across the water you are dark." Her poem "For War and Water" is a powerful update on the traditional lament about sons going to war.

> like my boy, born the year before
> cops killed even more black boys
> and more boys killed other boys
> for loving boys and more
> swastikas showed up on walls

If some of these poems sound dark, they are. But Dasbach manages a kind of hope. Not by offering false resolutions, but through the moral weight of her words and imagination. In "Inheritance" she gives us a transformative vision of her murdered great-grandfather.

> Wounded, pocked, shot through,
> he walks beside me now, so close,
> sometimes I think I feel his hand.
> His body glows with stars.

The Many Names for Mother brings us living history in beautiful, terrible complexity, a world "in flux like sand and water and ancestry."

—Ellen Bass

AFRAID ANCESTRAL

Mom is afraid

the sky will fall

because it's fallen

before

and there

is no recovering

from the weight

of clouds.

I. Drowned

AGAINST NAMING

Let's not name her or compare
flesh to fruit. Let's joke instead
how she swallowed a seed and let it
grow inside her. Just imagine,
how heavy is that sound and what
it tastes like in ripe summertime heat.
I had no cravings though. Only wanted to touch
the cold or be touched. Polish berries carried
the winter, so I ate them by the bucket.
Gooseberries, currants, sour cherries, bursting
childhood in my mouth. A past made sweeter
by its being passed. My mother sweating through
tolkuchka—the little push 'n' shove bazar—
to return home with a stained skirt and fruit
dangling from her ears and me, hungry
inside her. The Krakow market was a harvest too
this hottest July on record and in Oświęcim, the camps
didn't know what to do with all the people
in such heat, so at the gates of Auschwitz
sprinklers appeared—for the children mostly.
And you, my love, were just about the size
of a heart inside me then, soft
and wanting. Water and a past
that isn't this. One not passed down.
But I carried you there anyway. Against
my family's urges. Against even your future
ones, maybe. Walked you miles across
black ground turned red then gray then left
for colorless. The dead beneath us
silent. The ones around us, growing.
And I sang to you of a golden city
under a paling sky with its magic garden
and single star and the flame-maned lion
waiting there. You listened, my love, perhaps
they did too, ashes rising in the creek and in the petals,
Birkenau's waters and purple wildflowers,

its big book of names
from which we did not choose
to name you. Valen, valiant, strong, unmarked
by ancestry or first generation or Slavic or fruit.
But V, for the survivor who refused
to be named that, for the numbered and unnumbered
names unwritten and scattered there, for the woman
who made seeds grow as gorgeous
out of flesh as out of stone.

FOR WAR AND WATER

Everyone is having boys, my mother says.
That means war is coming. The way
it came in the old country—boys
rising out of the ice and cold
potato fields, boys laying bricks
and digging, wells and trenches
and bodies—boys out of other boys
like my boy, born the year before
cops killed even more black boys
and more boys killed other boys
for loving boys and more
swastikas showed up on walls
and more walls went up, invisible, where
once ran rivers. But a river
is not a boy. A river can either
run dry or bleed and everyone
will blame someone
darker or an animal, that gorilla
who dragged away the little boy
or the gator who stole another.
But in the water, they seem
so strong, resilient even, these boys
born months apart, these boys
who suck the water down, who beat it
with their tiny fists and kick as though
they're running, these boys who grow
not knowing they were born for war
and that it's everywhere
and there is no
outrunning water.

about the hair, how it falls out, webs
between your fingers and streams
in the shower and clumps on your pillow
and on the floor and in the hands of one
who still loves you. They say it'll grow back.
Thicker even. But you don't believe them.
They've lied before. And they don't tell you
about the split, how you can fit
a fist between your left and right sides.
You can work to make it narrower, they say,
build back the muscles in your abdomen
and pelvic floor. It just takes time.
You can get it all back, they say, but you know
that is not the point. And you knew you'd be tired,
that the body can only keep up for so long.
They warned you days would be long but years
would fly and again, they were wrong,
because everything is flying and the rain
is coming down the way July had never known it.
And you think, my body was an ark once.
And you ask, would it still float? And in days,
your son will have breathed air as long as water.
And maybe Noah was a woman too.
They never told you this. But the rain
is coming and you are holding
a wad of your own hair in one hand
as your son's head rests along the other.
And you think, they never told you
any of this. How your hands
would never keep up.

LETTER TO MY SON

On his 1st birthday, November 8th, 2016

Remember, here you are a white man
—pearl bone tooth pillowcase linens cotton mouth morning—
but only here.
Know, across the water you are dark
—soil branch riverbed blackbird blood bruise mouth mourning—
you are otherness among others and among yours.
Remember, they won't see it here at first.
They'll call you by your given name.
They'll hold your hand and ask
to hear your history.
They'll listen as generations
slip from your tongue—
                          soiled bones and teeth and linens mouths—
a shower of stars made brighter
by galaxies gone dark. They'll trust you
when you say your pockets are empty,
but I'll have taught you to always carry stones,
to save them for graves
because you never know
when you'll walk among the dead,
because you'll know
they're everywhere.
But remember, here
you are a white man
the dead under
                    your skin   your feet   inside   your mouth.
They crack your white bones
milk teeth   raw gum line   still sealing soft spot.
They whisper, *you were never one of us*, and hold you
to their chest to sink you into ground.
But remember, little sun, you are more
than stone or pearl or star or mineral,
more than body or metaphor can make you

or color name you or land and water divide you
more than ma or man or mine.
You will know our stories
in your bones
                    —branch   black sea   bruised and blooming—
when neighborhood boys threw stones at your mother
and words at her mother and then hands at hers,
when they threw fists at your grandfather and bullets at his
and finally shoved your great-great-grandfather so far
beneath the earth, no stone or throw could reach there,
you will know that none of us
were white men then. Remember,
when half of your ancestors died, the other half
did the killing. Remember, murderer and murdered
are just one death apart and your skin too
is translucent, kin on its underside, kin just one
sibilance away. Remember how much this matters
everywhere, how skin hurts, how no love is deep enough
to forget this and no skin thick enough to endure.

mother is born from "a thick substance
concreting in liquors," like the whiskey
they tell you to rub on new gums or the red wine
my mother told me would help his forming heart
grow stronger, *Look how resilient you turned out,* she says,
not knowing she too comes from "lees" or "scum" or "waste
of skin," probably from Middle Dutch *modder*
"filth and dregs," what's left of us after
we've been named, but also see *mud,* found in many
words denoting "wet" or "dirty" or "damp" or "moist"
and other women tell you how they hate
the sound of it, without explaining why, that word
between the thighs, how they would rather come
from Old Irish *muad* for "cloud," would rather look up
in wonder, counting cows or crows or clowns, imagining
their bodies too can change back just as easily, can shift
from solid into air then back to water, without coming
from the Polish *mul* "slime," the Sanskrit *mutra-* "urine"
other women don't tell you is okay to talk about and be and let
release without becoming "excrement," without relief being
related to the German *Schmutz* "dirt," but your son's hands
are full of it, the scum and dregs and filth, the earth he shovels
in his mouth, devouring the world both of you come from,
moving from mud to mouth to you so easily, you realize
that being named for the "lowest or worst of anything,"
in his hands, is as close as you can get to flying.

Toilet paper wings
trailing behind him, my son
flaps through the house.
He's unraveled the entire roll
in seconds, that's all it took
to leave so much white behind,
on the floor and in the air
and in his hands. That's how he burned,
I think, Icarus that is, but my son
isn't reaching for the sun yet
and I haven't taught him intent,
that arms transform
when they move that quickly,
that the body is always just an instant
away from becoming
something else, from leaving
the ground or returning to it.
And he falls, on his knees
or face, flat to the hardwood, falls
without knowing how
it happened and rises
having forgotten he ever fell.
Maybe we need that too, to forget
or fall more, to move against
the past instead of towards it,
because underwater, the wax
must have congealed
back to wings around him
as the backwards sun
swallowed the whole
bird of him, clouds and body
strewn inside out,
left white and bare
as the hottest part
of a dying flame
or a star maybe,

one we watch night after night,
forgetting it must have died
so long ago
to still trail the sky.

GENESIS

The sky in June
rises with horns,
my grandmother's
about her neck in gold,
and sets with chelae, claws,
pincers, the many names

for mother.
A bull gives birth
to a crab, a crab to a ram,
a ram to the cusp
of scorpion and centaur—
the sky grows full
with parturition.

How many names
for this? The looking up.
The summer stars
and all their distant
meaning. The many
names for mother.

How animal
to fit inside
another
and human
to tear our way
back out.

WIKIPEDIA FOR "NAME"

1. Etymology
from father to father to farther away
from the father or take the mother instead
and keep her where she belongs
under a name that isn't hers

2. In religious thought
see "Names of God"
and then refuse
to write them down
and ask if ink
is sacrilege or faith

3. Names of names
person / body / anthroponym / another body / hold me as if I'm yours
place / please / toponym / top of a mountain / toppling down
body of water / body of body / hydronym / hear me under / drowning
ethnic group / not mine / ethnonym / still not / mine? / I don't
    understand the question
resident(s) of a locality / locusts / demonym / demon / demand return
    / anywhere   but home
false name / face / hand / rib / pseudonym / pass
named after a person / below earth / below water / below skin /
    eponym / upon   the grave

4. Further reading
my mother was afraid
and made my father
take her name
and so my husband was afraid
and made me take his
and so I was afraid too
and made our son
take my great-grandmother's
and so she turned

scared in her grave
the stones above her
shook and called out
for god to give it back

LEARNING YIDDISH

To Vikhlya Moishka Gershkovna Khalfin 1912–2003

Vera, though I never called you that, you,
babushka, groys bubby, mamen, whose name
in Russian rings of faith, in Yiddish
of debate, in Latin it is all that's true,
though other romance tongues have argued you
claim impartial judgment like a god.
Then, in the German, Vera is a strong,
wild boar, sowing the fields your yellow hue.

But when I searched the Hebrew, you floated
up out of the letters of your own
Talmudic name: *vav vav yud resh aleph,*
two hooks, wisdom, beginning or a head,
then teacher. Vera, let me say your name again—
Which tongue do I believe? And which did you?

I.

She doesn't remember,
but I woke one morning
to her pounding, boring

holes in the wall
with the black tip
of her cane.

She'd trapped herself
inside the bathroom,
the cane hovering

like the nose
of an unnamed fish
about to fall

out of the drywall.
She was still mumbling,
"Gotteniu tayer. Gotteniu

vey zmir," and my foreign
words to calm her,
"There's no one there,"

stuck to the walls.
In her flowered robe,
she sat on the toilet.

Vera doesn't remember,
but this is how I found her:
wet and swollen varicose legs

submerged in fabric,
like humpback whales
unable to come up for air.

II.

In languages we could not understand,
and then again for all of us to hear

and comprehend, she screams
about his filthy hands and how she'd never

let them touch her where she'd already been touched
by warmer hands that never lit a match

nor pressed it to the body of a living man.
Does she remember or imagine him? The beast

that kicked flesh with a hunter-green boot
into a hole full of half-live bodies: men, trapped

between sleep and death; men, waiting
to be set on fire with their brothers; one man,

most tender, whose hands still dream to hold
her hands and wield her cane and shoot.

III.

I'm told she wasn't always like this.
Told by others like my *mamen* and hers,
told her legs were thinner, hair was darker,

and lips, always red. I'm told that even
during war, when they dyed her yellow
and worked her raw, even after, when

my father had to lift her across
the Atlantic to a land she'd only heard
was warmer and freer and more colorful

in the fall, even then, she took the time
to put on lipstick, the bright red kind
that leaves smudges on men's shirt collars.

IV.

One night, back
in the motherland,
her husband

did not return, so
she walked barefoot
through the grasslands,

following dry drops
of blood encased
in hoof prints.

She found
a moose head,
his nose still warm,

still melting
the surrounding snow.
Her body fell to him,

inhaling rusty iron
mixed with mane.
He would come back to her

across the decades,
warm, still
with his half-live

lurking eyes, though
all the rest of us
were blind.

V.

What if that morning smelled
not quite how I remembered?

Maybe you got out the broken soviet
samovar to make chamomile tea

and let the smoke creep up
the stairs under my sheets

to wake me. Were lemons
cut to perfect circles and placed

around a gold-rimmed plate
with *pryaniki* and sour cream

and so much sweet yellow glow
that you made the entire kitchen

grow together into you, until
I couldn't tell the scents apart?

And now even my husband smells of you,
or something flesh-like I remember.

But memory's a wild and fragile thing,
it's glass we shattered under the chuppah.

And he's a German, did I tell you that?
His last name pounds like hands

striking a keyboard – Bach, Bach, Bach!
Were you playing his name that morning

against the wall, sounding out
his syllables with your cane, calling

for him to rescue you with his name?

VI.

Sasha, was his name, и она его любила,
her daughter tells, over the last of kindzmarauli.

He didn't drink and his clothes smelled of smoke
from the ironing board. I saw her take his hand, the first man's

she'd touched since—more wine, she lets it overflow.
Blue eyes, too blue to be like ours, they showed

a coast I'd never seen. I dream about them sometimes.
I look away. *She never married him you know,*

но она его любила. On my pillow, blond-
haired, blue-eyed, he left the only doll I ever had,

and while I held her plastic body, my mother pushed
him out the door.

VII.

They say, when her husband was sent to Siberia,
she refused to stay in their brick apartment.
She traveled first by rail, then by wagon,

to the land of no women and no heat,
only ice and mercury, where convicts
were once patriots and clay huts

once were homes. They say she gave birth
to her first girl there, on an oven or a bathroom
floor or in their straw-stuffed bed.

They say she screamed for water
and neighbors came running and then
she screamed for more, and I believe them.

VIII.

Simcha, the prize,
the beloved, the listener,
the boundary for one
or all of us. His name
is not carved into a plaque
lit up by an eternal flame,
nor did we find it
in a book that lists
all those who burned
or fell away from bone.
When I read you the list
of Babi Yar victims
and his nomen was missing,
did you remember
your return to Kiev?
The unburied city
where nooses swung
suspended from trees
and telephone poles,
where handmade ropes
strangled the breath
from necks in uniform,
left men dangling for days
while survivors watched
December's frost flake away
and take the hanged men's skin.
Men who wouldn't be laid
to rest in breadbasket soil
alongside the thousands
they heaved into it.
Vera, you had no place
to pray over the loss
of unrecorded body.
Even from the American coast,

I see the dust that looms
above that frozen ground: living
entombed beneath the dead.
If only their breath
could melt the deepening snow,
show us where to dig
for all the missing,
and let your daughter
stop waiting
for her father
to come home.

IX.

These belonged to you, Vera: the heads and blood,
those moose you said were hanging from the walls;
the precious teeth hidden in a glass of murky water,

never safe from Nazi thieves; white sleeping pills
you thought we secretly snuck into dog food
to keep the German shepherd guard from waking us

when men in green would come for you; your walker
with its worn-down tips and rusted legs; and your hands
with their fortune creases, they're gone—all gone now.

My fast for you on Yom Kippur: twenty-five hours
without food or drink or washing or sex—thinking
of you and God. You walking towards Him

through the kitchen, convinced the lit gas stove
was the burning bush whispering, *Take off
your shoes.* But our house, this land

we took you to, uprooted from black earth
where your body could have slept in wheat fields,
this house, our house, was never your holy ground.

II. Light

THE MOON IS SHOWING

her naked butt-side
as I walk home
asking, what is poetic
about the moon or back?
The hung-open sky
is everything & nothing
like moon or body because
it's always poetry when you say
body or moon & when you say butt
the music splits inside & the moon
broke so long ago, we've forgotten.
So why is there a pleasure
in the wronging or the being
wronged? The toughness
in my great-grandmother's tongue
was like two moons once, avocado
& its seed, swallowing
generations to bear
more broken moons
& when my love
grabs my ass so hard
I think I feel his hands
reach the place where once
I carried life, I can't help looking
to the sky, mouth waxing, body
both the crater & the rock, body
both the birth & birthing, body because
when I say my my   my enough,
my body enough,   possession realigns,
when I say my body, my ba ba ba   body,
I hear my Babas
who told me, *your behind
is dirty,* told me, *poetry
is clean* & shining & not
about the body, told me, *yours
is not a place that one should touch,*

& taught me touch
is everything & touch
is love & touch is what the moon
is made of, so when my love
touches my ass & I admit
I like it, the shame of it,
the dark side & the light, shame
the waxing reach, shame
the opening & everything
it carries, life
& shit & shit
inside of life &
when my son came out of me
they feared he had already taken
a shit inside, but the first thing to emerge
was not a scream, the first,
from his two, tiny showing
butt-sides was shining,
black coal, a stone,
a poem, a body,
a brazen new moon
out of the old.

OTHER WOMEN DON'T TELL YOU

you will forget
someone's birthday
your son's   winter coat
at his grandparents'   when the weather turns   cold
his fingertips   and they aren't blue
but a color   for which there is
no name   like the pain
of childbirth   which they say   you will forget
but you remember   every splitting   of your body
and instead   forget the way   your people suffered
saying   there is   no language   for the cold   they bore
no language for   forgetting
and yet you manage it   so easily
the way you fall asleep   the way
the crescent moon   hangs in the sky
like a closed eyelid   the way its sliver
sunk snuck in   even after   you'd forgotten it
the way you forget   forgetting
keep using   the same word
despite its lack   of meaning   and you tried
to go and buy   a new coat
one that would fit   your son's   long torso
his arms   stretching to his knees
but other women
didn't tell you   how he would grow
immeasurable   the black sky   at once
everywhere and nowhere   the full
moon and the new   and everything
that you've forgotten   of that cold and night
of language   your people's   birth-
and death-days   frozen in his bones
though already   the days grow longer now
by minutes only   like his legs
more ready to walk away

Because she wore cherries in her ears
instead of gold or stone or silver.

Because hers were heavier than fruit.
Because they made me want

milk we didn't have. Because
of want. Because I couldn't fit

the word, *zhem-choog*, in my mouth
and all that white reminded me too much

of teeth. Because we threw teeth
behind the stove so new ones

would grow in. Because sometimes
they didn't. Because change is the only

certain beauty and strung up
side by side, things ceased to be

as beautiful. Because holding
failed across continents and my mother's

jewelry box stayed empty. Because leaving
meant she could only take one

necklace. Because the pearls, like teeth,
were left behind.

MY MOTHER AS A FAILED SONNET, OR MAYBE JUST A FOREST

I've written you as rivers, as frost, as everything
hidden underneath it, as a children's picture
book in a foreign language, as language, that one and all
others, as your hands and those of your mother and
hers, most often hers, as what she held in them, as
the empty tea kettle, as everything she'd lost, the dead
and their sea and its unsinking, as salt, as what abandon
must mean and what it must taste like, war
and famine, immigration and tea,
Ceylon, Lady Gray, Darjeeling, as the fortune
it leaves at the bottom of spent cups, and as
those cups, carried across ocean and name, as water,
generations and generations of it, mothers'
open hands, as bare Russian birch branches
grasping for clouds, as what a child sees
looking up in a forest.

WHY DO GIRAFFES CLIMB TREES?

Because acacia is sweetest
at the canopy and grows

more beautiful
when viewed from above.

Because no two giraffes
or trees have the same

pattern, coat or bark
or branch or hoof, and no two

clouds look the same
from below and no two

giraffes can climb
the same tree or reach

the clouds. Because we too
can't help looking up and

when we can't see,
we climb. Because giraffes learn

falling from birth. Because
of mothers. And the heart.

Because theirs is the largest
of any land mammal and weighs

24 pounds and pumps
60 gallons of blood a minute.

Because they don't keep
such records

or remember the trees
they've climbed. And because we

are born remembering
to scream, while they

are born knowing
to stand.

MICROSATELLITES

Great-grandmother dreamed there were
two of you inside, two scorpions locked
by their tails, exoskeletons on fire, one
wearing great-grandfather's face, she forgot
the other but remembered two mouths
exhaling water, *I kissed them,* she told me,
all four cheeks, she saw both of you split
the sky where you hunt the hunter and burn
eternal, felt both of you move, siblinged
under my skin, but in waking, we heard
one heartbeat, saw one skeletal outline,
more water than body, more animal
than arachnid, all you, untwinned, *I was stung
twice,* she said, and I asked her
if it hurt, *only the first time,* but the stars
never stop hurting.

TAKE AN X-RAY OF THE SUN, YOU'LL FIND

a Rainier cherry
at its yellow heart, fire
skinned and ripe

with reaching.
But in the sunless
lush green mosses

where the fruit
is born, bucketfuls
of sweetness

only bring to mind
vareniki s vishnami,
cherry dumplings,

made on a board
over the bathtub
we called a kitchen table.

I watched my mama work
flour deep into the dough,
her nails a darker red than

chernacorka, black-rind,
sour cherries,
that only grow

out of Ukrainian soil
and taste, or tasted once,
like the inside

of sunlight, or
its saccharine glow
fighting to get out.

MOTHER'S 20-YEAR-OLD MATTRESS

Inside: springs : wood : lint : moths : hair : spiders :
          cotton : condoms : salt : sweat : spit : so much
               skin : blood : tea : cough syrup : carbonated water :
          carbon : honey : paper : nails : nicotine : polish : ash : nitrogen:
               the Russian red-gold wedding band she wore
          until it wouldn't fit her swelling

On top: the body America gave her : heavy : soft :
          sinking : her back rounding metal and fabric
               to canoe : her back won't float : aching
          from the past : aching for it more : they're doing
               x-rays she told me : waves and waves:
          she's always drowning in the dreams : the pain
               is never there when I wake up she says :
          insists it's not the mattress : refuses something new :
               tells me to stop blaming surface :
          anxiety and immigration : tells me I don't know how
               to pity her : if my body can bear she says :
          a body : an ocean : this bed can keep on bearing mine

Underneath: the sales receipt
          for Sealy Beautyrest
          Plush Pillowtop Queen
          delivery included

          as a child she slept
          on a wooden board
          for her scoliosis
          woke broken

          termites in her hair
          under her nails
          between her gums
          her mouth a bed

never again she said
will anybody tell me
what I must bear
beneath me

Yuuuuooona, he calls, pointing up and drawing
out the *ooo*, the Russian "L," still
too hard to form "Luna."
We understand, make meaning
out of what its left us: *Yuuuuooona,*
on the shoulder of my shirt
where his sleeping mouth's wet outline
left imperfect waning, *Yuuuuooona,*
in the fabric covering my belly, where
his finger found a hole through which
skin shone like moonlight, *Yuuuuooona,*
on the wings of every moth or butterfly,
Yuuuuooona, more Yuuuuooona, our cats' eyes
twinkling in darkness, spinning spheres
he is still too slow to catch, *My Yuuuuooona,*
in the daylight's glare, he names the sun
as his, asks it to come closer, and opens wide
to hug, to swallow, to hold
its unfathomable glow, and in the water too,
in any water, *Yuuuuooona, Yuuuuooona,*
bath, puddle, lake, sea, ocean, rain,
our faces and the light, a river, and
in the window, any window, especially
a stranger's, *Yuuuuooona,* this December,
morning, through smoking sky
and a cobweb of trees, he finds it there,
even as it fades, and in my pocket,
I find it too, *Yuuuuooona,* an envelope
of his first-trimmed crescent hairs,
so many fallen moons.

III. Animal

OTHER WOMEN DON'T TELL YOU

what your mother will say
just after he is born, after they slap him
onto your stomach like a wet rag, the tether
binding you still warm and pulsing,
and just as you look down, expecting blood,
they don't tell you sometimes it isn't there,
the flesh, almost clean, dark moss of hair
covered by a thin white film, a second skin,
a part of you still holding him, perhaps.
He looks like an alien, she exclaims, giddy
with becoming, but they tell her she's too young
to be a grandmother and she is happier for it.
Are his ears going to stay like this? As if she'd never
given birth herself, though she reminded you
she has, just hours earlier, your belly rising
like a moving mountain as she recalled
how back in the old country, she was stitched up
with nothing for the pain. The young male nurse
responded to her screams, *Does it really hurt*
that bad? And other women tell you
that it does. That it's unbearable
but you will bear it. That it's a mountain
and drowning. That it's all worth it
in the end. They don't tell you when
the pain really comes, when it moves
through you, a rush of snowmelt
boring boulders on the side of the road
and everyone stopping to look, that a small part of you
will love the feeling, the control to grind
as though you were chewing stones, the want
to bear the way centuries have, bare
and unbroken by the bearing, like the women
who didn't tell you any of this. Your grandmother
or hers, holding each other, hands
and boiling water and sopping towels and feeling
everything, only to never speak about their pain.

To continue having girls.
To raise them so they know
to let their mothers be a part
of everything. To understand your mother
when she reminds you that you are an only child
because your tiny body hurt her
bad enough to never want for more.

THE QUESTION

In the voice of my mother

It always gets out: my foreign voice and name
they can't quite place. *Russia,* I say
because Ukraine would lead to more confusion.
Why did you come to America? They ask
and I change the subject or leave
the room. For my daughter, this
is not interrogation but permission
to tell *her* story without shame, heavy
and sour, no judgment for being
what we are, because most
can't hear it
                    when she speaks.

Is the only difference in our accounts
accent and accent-less? Is hers more vivid?
Its gaps filled in by years of stories.
So young, she never could have seen
the places cast now in a worded half-light.
Still, she captures them and calls it
art, calls it poetry, calls, without
hearing me say: *I lived that thing you like to reimagine—*

In Kiev: the train station, detail-less, save
for its wash of white, bunk beds, crying there
with all the will and wildness of a child, and all
the childish reasons or their lack, because
she had to leave behind a life-size doll
that walked beside her when she held its hand.
Flying, family she'd never known, and soon
forgot, more flying, sleep, lights, but she remembers
them: the flashes of pictures when keeping
eyes open was harder than standing; the glowing
house with a giant bowl of pears, bananas

and fruit she'd never tasted in winter; and that couch,
where she fell asleep, only to wake screaming.

But what of the looks?
How they scoured our clothes for gold
until I was lucky to keep my wedding band.
The fortune it took to get out, seven Jews
(unheard of), young, old and older, armed
only with our red passports, inspected for hours
at the customs gate where we never heard
the English words we'd learned: *welcome home.*

JOKES DON'T TRANSLATE WELL
FROM RUSSIAN

It goes something like, there was once an alcoholic, because
it always starts with drinking, and his wife, because every husband

must come with one, and she of course wants him to quit
and wears robes and makes tea, constantly, serving

sweets and preserves and sour cream, always sour cream,
my mother tells us over wine and tea and sweets, and yes,

sour cream because coming from Ukraine, it is even more certain,
and the preserves are always cherry, but back to this wife,

her friend advises her to fill a bathtub to the brim
with vodka and then throw in a dead cat, your husband

will be so disgusted, she says, that he'll never drink again,
my mother finishes her white, the red gives her headaches now,

or an upset stomach, or some other pain, a sobering
one she discovered in America, then she tells the unworthy boy

I brought home, my husband years of drinking later,
that the secret to keeping a woman happy

is to always keep

her glass full, so he does this, and the wife too does
as she's told, then leaves the house, how easy

it must have been to find dead cats back there and then,
when she returns later that night, everything is quiet,

no stumbling or snoring, no bottles or body on the floor,
she goes into the kitchen, my mother holds her breath,

and I jump in to clarify why, that bathtubs were often
in kitchens and multipurpose, ours would be covered

with a wooden board and transformed to a makeshift table
for cutting potatoes and kalbaska and onion or anything

boiled or pickled, soon be doused in mayonnaise and garlic,
or yes, sour cream, but this wife sees that the bathtub

is empty, and the husband is wringing out
the cat and whispering, *nu kiska, nu izhio chut' chut'*,

this part doesn't sound as good in English, she says,
kitty, a little more, no a few more drops is better, and then

my mother takes the empty bottle and wraps her fingers tight
around the glass, mimicking the wringing motion, this is how

we squeeze everything until the last drop, she says, the dead
are no exception.

Every fairy tale, another stepmother
    tries to kill her children.
Starve or burn or bury them
    in locked rooms and dark woods
and ovens, and you recall your history
    is one of ovens, so when your son
tries to climb inside, you worry
    about his willingness.
And every news story, another
    mother loses her first born—
a car crash or crime or accident.
    The past, a book of mothers
trying to unlearn how hatred
    festers in the blood
and passes down. How hatred blooms
    on skin, inside the mouth
a bursting poppy. How made
    of flesh, it even looks
a lot like love at first—
    your son's great-great-
grandmother's for the man
    she'd never marry
because he wasn't lined up in a row
    next to her husband
nor made of seed and chernozem
    nor marked
for hatred. So she passed it
    on to you, and your son too
will find it, reaching out
    for his reflection, his shadow
in a field of wildflowers.
    He will trace it in contours
that seem too small
    to bear such feeling,
and when he looks at you, you'll know
    there is so little you have done
to teach him this, but not enough
    to help unlearn.

it will always be your fault:
his nose running
after that first dip
in the Atlantic,
his bruised elbow
and scraped knee,
his hair, too long,
always in his face
and his face, too much
or too little of yours,
his hard hands
slapping the animals,
unclear, misshapen
words, loud and large enough
to fill any public space
with unintelligible language,
and then that birthmark,
high up on his glute,
that one's especially
your fault, from when
you were so scared
you grabbed
onto your belly—fear
seeps through the fingertips,
your mother said, down
into thick, pregnant flesh,
down through fluid
and layers of your body
protecting his, down
onto unknowing skin—
marking him afraid,
the history he comes from,
in perpetual, dark bloom

EVERYONE IS TERRIFIED FOR THEIR KIDS

because the world keeps ending & ending
    without end & this winter
    the dead
    leaves remain here
    to remind us
    what is happening
because it keeps happening & there's blood
    on the moon & in the water &
    on someone's hands
because of our hands
because a kid not old enough
    to drive or smoke or drink or reach
    the top shelf
    can still reach
    the gun & shoot
because he will & the will
    to bear arms is strong
    in our country
because of bears & arms & children & all
    their terrified animal bodies
because my son says
    Scare me! & grabs
    my neck & digs in & asks
    for growls & roars & claws
    asks me to jump out
    from behind the walls
because we raise our kids
    with terror
    in their bones now
because *Scare me, Mama!* means
    he is already
    afraid & wants
    again & again
    to feel it
because what else
    is left

WHILE EVERYTHING FALLS APART, IMAGINE HOW YOU'LL TEACH YOUR SON ABOUT DEATH

when he rips a dandelion head off its stem
and wonders why the body shrivels
or the pregnant stray gives birth
to her calico litter and you find two of them
wedged underneath your car tires that winter
when the drunk woman across the street falls
leaving parts of herself down every row house stair
last night's howling in her lungs and on your windows
and the neighbors drape her body well
before the ambulance arrives
he will ask where they've all gone and why
look up instinctively and wonder
and you'll confess you do not know
hold him and say nothing
about elsewhere being better or everything
happening for a reason
you'll hold him as though your hands
could weigh him down
could keep his bones from growing
as the clouds move slow
he'll notice for the first time
they are white "Not blue?"
he'll ask surprised and you will nod
say something about the shapes of animals
then he'll remember the flower and kittens
the dead woman
                              "Will they come back?"
and you'll again stay silent
because the lawn is full
of broken glass and water bottles
full of piss and dog shit full
of yesterday and you will shake
your head and think you're doing right by him
it's better he know now you tell yourself
and watch him look away and up
search for the dead inside the clouds

WHILE EVERYTHING FALLS APART, IMAGINE HOW YOU'LL TEACH YOUR SON WHERE HE COMES FROM

use objects they tell you
precise and tangible
a material body
he can hear and touch
a seashell singing of its mother's
black-sea-boned skin
a dry flower from the Caspian steppes
still in the midst of dying
a reminder of this his Earth
so you try to give him the Earth
coming from nowhere
and everywhere at once stolen
stones and sand from the Coliseum
a stranger's grave
no one's home
a field of missing material
bodies so you try to give him yours
or at least an imprint
the face you made
on matte in black and white
holding a wheat stalk
posing as a good child
against a grown-up wind
and when his father names you
Ukrainian names you
by where you come from
you don't correct him
and know your son
will never understand
you pray he never has to
unsure what language
god can hear or feel
you wish to give your son
the giant bear with one

button-eye and the other
a knot that held your mother
when she was scared and far too small
to get her arms around
its overbearing body
it's in the sea and steppe
along with all the rest
in stone and sand in soils
whose names are foreign now
so you give your son your hands
and let his fingers trace
their lifelines because the only
stuffed animal you have
reeks of chicken soup
and someone else's childhood
but your hands are his
to keep to keep to keep
on coming from

WHILE EVERYTHING FALLS APART,
IMAGINE HOW YOU'LL TEACH YOUR
SON HE IS AN ANIMAL TOO

as he hugs the dog with his whole body
his weight on top of her not knowing
his own strength or knowing it
far too well
as he weaves his arms
into a snare around her neck to show it
and after he's thrown all his food
to the ground or hovered it
right in front of her nose
he yells *no eat no eat iya* making the "n"
in front of her name silent
because he's still learning
to speak or already knows silence
helps her hear the *no's* as harsher
already finding it easy
to claim something as his, *my iya,* everything
as not hers or yours and how easy it is
to learn superiority without being taught it
or have you been teaching him all along
how easily he loves her and knows too
he is above that kind of love

WHILE EVERYTHING FALLS APART, IMAGINE HOW YOU'LL TEACH YOUR SON ABOUT LOVE

repeating *gentle, gentle,* remind him
how to touch and not bite back
when he's intent to leave

his teeth inside

to take your hair with him to bed
and keep on screaming
for even more of you

when there's so little left
the bears sleep warm inside the earth
you sing *so close* they cannot tell

where one's skin ends and soil begins
the trees reach for the moon you sing
and all the birds sleep warm and quiet

you hold him still
against your chest and lips
against his will sometimes and hum

lost yiddish of the small boy
orphan selling *papirosm, koyft she*
koyft she, papirosm to get warm

or of the russian beggar girl
with her *garyachi bublichki*
as the unbearable night moves in

like a train against the dying
oil lamp *bublichki garyachi*
bublichki hot rings of dough

the name you called him
when he grew that hot
and round inside your belly

you taste them as you sing
and as you kiss his father
long and hard and every time

you speak of love

you mean it—*lyblyu libe libe*—
and every time your son extends
to a hug stranger

you're afraid *the cradle*
will rock and grateful
the wind blows afraid

always afraid *the bough*
will break every time he reaches
with the whole of him

you wonder if he learns
through the vibrations
between your mouths

if he noticed the woman
begging you for money
had no teeth

if he heard her singing
squeezing your stroller-
wielding arm *gentle, gentle,*

singing *baby, darlin' thank you*
for your smile, for believing her
the big night stirs snow

with a spoon you sing
your neighboring bears
swim beside the moon

you sing you sing

so when his mouth opens
it will be full
gentle, gentle, animal

WHILE EVERYTHING FALLS APART, IMAGINE HOW YOU'LL TEACH YOUR SON ABOUT GUNS

bang, bang, he asks every night, *bang, bang,*
and you're dead, wants you to sing in his ear
bang, all the ways we know how to take

each other's lives and all the tools we've made
to help us do it, he forms tiny fists pretending,
already knows his body is enough, *bang, bang*

and when you take away his neon water gun,
he cries and throws his head back on the pavement,
bang, all the ways we know how to take

things away from children, to give them
back once they know how to really use them,
bang, bang, he asks every night, *bang, bang?*

outside your window and on the news,
in the small hands of his friends, their mouths,
bang, all the ways we know how to take

their hands and mouths for granted,
you're dead, a refrain so familiar it fires
soundlessly, *bang, bang,* every night, he sings
all the ways we know how to take.

IV. Drowned Animal of Light

OTHER WOMEN DON'T TELL YOU

it's a battle for the body, for every
part of it, *he's all you,* some say,
he has your eyes, and others, *he has
your hair, look at those curls,* and you let them
twist around your finger, vine tendrils
more plant than boy, more wild than will,
more him than you, but it's a battle
for ownership, for claiming the body
you left him with as yours, and when
you tell your mom he rode the escalator,
repeating "Whoaaaaa" in fascination
at each descent away from the fluorescence
until the lights of Gucci and Versace
drew him towards their dazzle, she says,
He has good taste, then adds, *You used to
have taste too.* So now you lack the parts
you've given him. You're blind,
chasing a toddler through the shopping mall.
You're Tiresias, prophet between earth and myth,
god and manlike thing, you've given everything
away to own these parts of him, the certainty
that they are yours, or so they've told you.
But you are eyeless and bald and he is full
of sight and mane and beautiful, and soon,
your mother says, she won't know how
to talk to you, but also, that he doesn't have
your mouth, his nose, she adds, is undecided still,
unclear if he will wear your history of bones,
dead noses piling up, all yours yours yours,
but maybe, not his, maybe, other women tell you,
he looks just like his dad, and you see it
in his cheeks and jawline, in the flatness
of his feet, the ankles caving in, and in the dips
from waist to hind, as though
some god or ghost has left
their thumbprints to remind you
how his body
isn't yours at all.

NAMES OF *SVET*

I. Sima

They left his baby girl   on the top bunk   beside an open window
and when he touched the glass   it burned   on both his palms
her red cheeks growing redder   in the sun
and he thought   she might catch on fire
so he could take a part of her   to where all ash
                                                            is human
where he could watch   the freckles on her face   take shape
imagining   how light is born   inside the body
and as the train pulled away   his fingers
left wet streaks   across his daughter's eyes   trying
to close them   before she could grow up
and see   her father
                                    disappear.

II. Marina

There was too much light   too much light
for her to stay above the water
so she and her mother hid under the blue
and the dark seaweed   closed around them
like shade   bound them at first
painted dolls   strung together in a breathless dance
then, the master's hand pulled up
                                    the mother's face
burned in the open air   but the girl stayed dancing
underwater a wild catfish   tangled in broken whiskers
until you couldn't tell them apart   from flesh
and the girl sucked in the salt   stiff   it turned her
into the swaying coral below   then she sank through the sand
sprouting wet roots   while above
stingrays opened their water-wings   veiled her
until others dug her out   dragged her   so she could lie
face-up   on the black soil   half-sea half-earth
open-mouthed   to swallow the sun.

64

III. Rima

The glaring headlights lifted three of them
like waves   above the smiling city
and eighteen stories up   they floated   holding hands
before the fall   to what was never water.

The mother's body broke   pieces of glass inside a kaleidoscope
and she slept for months   never dreaming
that both her wingless children   hovered in New York City's dust.

Scattered now   along the path she walks   and in the clouds
she searches for their faces   but there is nothing
but yellow light   the weight of both their palms
growing her down   pressing her into a barren earth

inside her belly   for centuries pregnant   they grow again
ghost limbs   with new eyes that never saw   a mother turn to stone
new shoulders   that never knew   the lack   the want
                                     of wings
new children   they do not try to fly
or seek to learn
                      the history of dying.

DIAGNOSIS: TAKOTSUBO

I'll die if you don't return, mother tells me,
like the beast to the girl in that old story,

with the wilting flower and dying father.
I'll die, she reminds me, almost daily

now that I'm already gone. But children
never believe such things—that one day, sooner

even than we realize, we won't have someone
we can leave. I know slowly, it's already happening,

her heart expanding into a fishing pot, an octopus trap,
clay and rope submerged in seawater, sinking.

They call it broken, but the muscle is far too strong,
it grows—balloons and stretches—until the chest

cannot contain it, until the skin is calm horizon
and the animal beneath breaks through the water,

open-mouthed and not an animal anymore.

some days, washing out every bottle will feel
like enough, scrubbing the milk-rings until their white
is in your skin and under your nails, some days letting
the plastic dry until it shines like expensive China,
some days, cleaning the bathroom, that too will feel
like enough, when you're squatting on the floor
across from your son, making noises that are animal
and beast and mother in one, watching him
scrunch his face into a prune to make
those same sounds, some days, when he picks up
a magazine about wood building and stays seated and looks
so much like his father and grandfather and likely theirs
and you are there to see this, those days
feel like so much more than enough. But others,
most days even, after you've hidden
every roll of toilet paper and every
spillable and breakable and chokeable, after
you've folded and tucked and verbed
through the things other women told you
make you woman or warm or worn-out man or maybe
just womb, after you've done more with your body
than your body has ever done, nothing feels like

> anything at all.

AND EACH

and each and every
each and every inch
of each and every each
that can be named
as every each *who* so
much wants each naming
and every naming wants
to be an each
spanning so much
much more than inches
and the each of every inch

wants each and every naming

every time a name falls

on a body

or a body falls and

each of every

body's inches wants

a name

and everybody

inches towards

the only thing

contagious

more

than laughter

is grief.

Animality is a precondition of the human
and there is no human who is not a human animal.
   —Derrida

mother told me about the baby
elephant in the Chinese zoo

who was rejected by his mother and cried
for the next five hours. animal-well

of childhood. an animal of grief. I'm O
negative, I told her, the universal

donor. I'll need a shot on the 28th
week and another one after. to this

she warned me about the body,
poison in its lack, how mine

wasn't water, could reject
what it carries, attack

the blood. *Keep it*

secret, she said, like a scar
behind clothing. *Wear safety*

pins to pierce the evil eye, dull
metal fighting a stranger's

severe will. *Don't cut*
your hair, veins and skin

are keratin, a kerosene
that lines the light inside, that will

not let the water in. but when
Persephone was taken,

Demeter wept autumn rain,
and when her daughter stayed

away, the mother's tears froze
into ice caps, kept falling as hard

hail, silver sleet, or soft snow
when she grew too tired

to grieve. but the mourning
customs of elephants

surpass the gods and the young
returns to its mother's

corpse, inspects it with her trunk,
and learns how grief outlasts

the waxen body, how light
ignites such water into blood.

OTHER WOMEN DON'T TELL YOU

the next day will be harder.

He will cry more, much more

having learned what it means

to be apart. He will cling to you

like soaking clothing, and once

off your body, he will become

a fish wrenching back

towards water, your face

a fresh lake, his mouth

gasping to drink.

Other women don't tell you

apart

means a part of you

is always drowning.

THOSE WHO GIVE BIRTH TO GOATS

Only one out of ten people born in a year of the Goat finds happiness
(十羊九不全)
    —*Chinese folk saying*

Some would drown
theirs as soon as they
were born. *Luck won't come*

with age, they'd say,
and death in water
proved far easier

than milk. Some would
cut theirs out early
to change the animal

while others would stop
making love all together
and wait for the goat

to pass. *Give birth
under the horse,* they urged,
in its calla lily mouth

and mane of jasmine,
in brackish yellow heat.
A goat, they said, *is raised*

*for nothing more
than slaughter,* an arid field
of withered primrose.

But his heart
is nothing
like the sound

of goat or horse hooves.
Between breathing
and drowning, he listens,

silver and quiet, balanced
on the ribs
like on the ancient frame

of an unbuilt house.

V. Home Eternal, Rising

we watched for what felt like hours
through the chain-link fence
whose netting fit my son's
entire arm or just his lips and chin
his tongue stretched out to inhale
crushed bricks / wires / roots / someone's
dead plant / mud / bones / pets' or rodents' / maybe / their owner
the excavator's overgrown arm
scooped through grass and soil
as easily as skin   making room
for new construction that will tower
at least two stories above most
other houses on our block
yama / pit / hole / ditch / trench / crag / crater / *higher*
my son asks / ravine / hollow / *more* / *more* / his fingers climb
the fence / he is ecstatic / growing / a grave
the man in the backhoe's cab
tips his hat and smiles
waves as he thrusts
the whole machine forward
its giant tires swallowing mud on the brink
thick legs anchored deep to fight the fall
the bluff where silt slips down soil walls
crumbling as easily   as skin and in my mouth
I taste the rust
the lines and lines and lines   of bodies   missing
from this moment when my son's whole face
is pressed against a fence   ignited by the other side
and all that lies below
ya / I / me / myself /   / ma / mama / mammal / YAMA
he yells / *MAMA YAMA!* / they don't belong here / ghosts / bones
should have been left across the water / blacker soil / not this / not this /
        /   / red mud / not deep   enough / not past
enough / not enough / this / is not enough /
YAMA MAMA! / they don't belong / these sounds / so close
to llama / sharp and comic / comma / drama / I'm laughing / crying /

gagging / trauma / he can't get enough of it / *YAMA!* / the word / its earth
    sick to my stomach I tore his fingers
    loose from the dust and metal
    and we walked through fresh puddles and debris
    he found a string with two deflated green balloons
    yayas he calls them   the sound
    as far from *sharik* as this dugout is   from Babi Yar
    as he is from the ghosts he doesn't know
    he comes from   as this house is
    from the bones one which it sits

DYADYA VODA

my son calls any body
of water—man, mister,
uncle water, uncle sea, uncle
ocean, *dyadya*, not father
but close, though we
didn't teach him this.
Kinship, nature flowing
into family, vast
expanse into what is
already inside him.
Obnimi Dyadyu Voda,
he says, and wraps
his arms around the waves,
Hug Uncle Water, and he falls
flat onto the sand, palms
wide and sinking
as though into my body.
Your kid is beautiful,
a passerby says, *have
more, a whole litter, and if
you have them close together,*
his cheek is in the sand,
mouth full of salt,
What's one more?
Everything, I think and want
to hold him, but he is water
and no matter how wide
I stretch my arms, I cannot
hug or count, cannot
contain the whole of him.

Jesus walked
    on water's back
& Moses split
    the Red Sea's throat
& Poseidon was swallowed
    only to bleed out
into the oceans & flood
    our feet & your
little love hasn't heard
    these miracles yet
or wondered which
    to believe, hasn't seen
men or gods
    float, fall, or turn
themselves to water,
    but he already knows
his tiny body
    can do it all.
Knows the blades
    you strapped to his feet
are Mercury's wings
    & the rink is full
of older kids
    afraid to lose
their bodies, but your son
    fears almost nothing,
lets go your hand
    & presses his cheek
into the ice & scrapes its frost
    into his mouth & tastes
how he is made
    in its own image,
how he is all
    its liquid, gas, & solid
forms, its man-god Kings
    of Sea & Sky & Earth &

Animal inside. He takes
        the water in
the way you take
        in air. He falls
as easily
        as breathing.

BAB'E LYETO / БАБЬЕ ЛЕТО /

All-Hallows' / Old Wives' / St. Martin's /
Indian / Second Summer / the sun's
refusing change when even horses
turn to drink the leaves
and feel the stiffness swim
into their hooves
when children swim in anything
a fading puddle or forgotten sprinkler
a shadow on the heated pavement
the alley cats flee
to soak up what still lingers
an October that stains
my son's cheeks the color
fallen leaves should be
his bones refusing to slow
the way a horse's would
but his curly mane tangled
wild and equine like
an animal or woman
a Russian peasant *baba*
and these her shortening days
to flee the fields and lift
her skirt to soak her legs
in salted water while
the trout and horse meats cure
and the pattypan pickles and milk fats
separate in cheesecloths hanging
from her oven racks
god's gift to Poland they used to call it
but further east these weeks
of warmth and linger
must have been needed no less
so imagine my *babas* indoors
grandmothers of grandmothers
hardening in their bones
gasping for rain and chewing

on pine needles so today
my son could sprawl out
in a fountain and drink
the sun they left him

CAMP MEANS FIELD

means open   summer means temporary means   go there someday
I tell my son means   naming the sun and wild flower by color   burnt
blue means   doesn't exist in nature means   tasteless but blue means
camp and war   in the body means   adhering   to doctrine or cause
camp-fever   epidemic-fever   life-fever   never-burnt-down-
fever means   endless   means as far as the eye   can see   but what if
the eyes are gone and in their place are   flowers   means
in their sockets are stones   my son   a stone in my belly then
my ancestors   stones around us   means field of stones
is not camp   even if camp means field   means   I have to stop
writing stones carrying   throwing   burying stones weighing
the body down   with what it's lost
        flowers I say   camp means field   I say it again means
this isn't my meaning   my *lager'* lagging stone   means what can be
remembered or named means   lagged behind   means lagend without water
is still a field   growing largess to lagrima to grime   amalgam
of languages I don't know   what they mean or where   they come from
        but лагерь   means field because field means   everything
crammed below the earth means   things growing   out that were once
pushed down   camp means when I pushed my son   out of me
I felt   I'd birthed   a stone
flowers   loose in my moleskin   brought back from stone fields   means
the fields   we were pushed out from means the fields we were pushed into
means there is no camp to return to   but there is still a field   *polye*
margin square bent brim bound domain range   province provide expanse
expanding flat means   flat means   flattened earth of stones
        means stoned bodies or bodied stones   means when you hear
Holocaust   wholly burnt or burned whole   sacrifice by fire   burnt
offering   caustic whole   you don't hear   stones or fields or flowers
        mean you don't hear blue   because gone and gray and counted
weigh far more   and you don't hear   a name because there are
too many   or a body   because the same   means you hear in plurals
in bodies   you imagine them means magnitude and you weigh
how wrong it is   to figure them this way   their lack or lessening
means them as stones again or still   but when my son hears
holy and challah and cost   years and years from now   hears it

over breakfast with his family perhaps   he will hear   a field means
the ghost who lingers there   means   imagine   growing wild
chicory dog violets snow-drops baby blues as far   as the eye can see

INHERITANCE

I wish I remembered
my great-grandmother's gaze,
the time she spoke turned inward
beyond where we are so alike,
the first time she told the story.
The room too warm, too thick
with honeyed light, and I too young
for her to think that I was listening.
Her features wear me now—the mole
on my left shoulder, soft, uneven
hips—I see her husband
in them. They echo his final vestige.
Taken away from a kitchen in Kiev,
the last place he looked for her
before the neighbor whispered
zhid and their house was left
empty until the war ended
and great-grandmother came back
to mourn his unfound body, her
hollowed home, the city
                    where he may have died.
All her silences and stories, full
I grew with them, full I'll pass uncertainty
to my children, told or retold, history
or memory, until one, a fading pulsar, bleeds
between stellar glow and blackening sky.
And in that distance, who can tell
igniting times apart? The difference
between the lived and the passed down:
the sundial's shadow at noon?
                         I'm wishing
again   today   still   last night—
in flux like sand and water and ancestry.
I'm wishing for her to have told me
                              his name.
Wounded, pocked, shot through,

he walks beside me now, so close,
sometimes I think I feel his hand.
His body glows with stars. Blood stars.
In a voice without gender or race,
I hear him call. And I am one among
the many, a blood star, and my children.
We will be the passing of light, body to body.
We wear our people's blood and smear
the sky with it, so when the rest look up,
they too will see nothing   but faces in the clouds.

ACKNOWLEDGMENTS

My deepest thanks to the editors of the following journals where these poems first appeared. Without your encouragement and belief in my words, this book would not be possible.

32 Poems: "In Everything, He Finds the Moon"

Academy of American Poetry: "Letter to My Son" and "For War and Water" (reprint)

The Account: "While everything falls apart, imagine how you'll teach your son about death," and "My Mother as a Failed Sonnet, or Maybe Just a Forest"

The Adroit Journal: "Why I Never Wore My Mother's Pearls"

American Poetry Review: "Other women don't tell you [mother is born]," "Other women don't tell you [what your mother will say]," and "Other women don't tell you [it's a battle]"

Beloit Poetry Journal: "Camp means field" and "There is no name for this."

Best New Poets 2017: "Against Naming" (reprint)

BOAAT: "Wikipedia for 'Name'"

Boxcar Poetry Review: "While everything falls apart, imagine how you'll teach your son where he comes from"

Cherry Tree: "babe lyeto / бабье лето /"

CLEAVER Magazine: "*Dyadya Voda*"

Contrary: "Why do giraffes climb trees?"

DIALOGIST: "Diagnosis: Takotsubo" and "Other women don't tell you [some days]"

Four Way Review: "Other women don't tell you [you will forget]" and "Microsatellites"

The Greensboro Review: "The Book of Mothers"

Guernica Magazine: "Names of *Svet*" published as "Stories of *Svet*"

Half-Mystic: "While everything falls apart, imagine how you'll teach your son about love"

The Missouri Review Online: "The Question"

Midway Journal: "Genesis," "Those Who Give Birth to Goats" and "the mourning customs of elephants"

Muse/A Journal: "Other women tell you"

Muzzle: "Other women don't tell you [about the hair]"

Narrative Magazine: "Learning Yiddish"

New South: "Against Naming"

Poetry Daily: "Other women don't tell you [what your mother will say]" (reprint)

Poetry International: "For War and Water"

Poetry Northwest: "Take an x-ray of the sun, you'll find" and "Other women don't tell you [the next day]"

Poets Reading the News: "While everything falls apart, imagine how you'll teach your son about guns" and "Everyone is terrified for their kids"

Sixth Finch: "Jokes Don't Translate Well from Russian"

SWWIM Every Day: "Why Walk When We Can Fly"

TriQuarterly: "While everything falls apart, imagine how you'll teach your son he is an animal too"

Vinyl Poetry: "and each" and "Other women don't tell you [it will always be your fault]"

Waxwing: "The moon is showing" and "Mother's 20-year-old Mattress"

I feel immeasurably overwhelmed with gratitude to so many people, I must first apologize to anyone I inadvertently forget to acknowledge by name. Know that if you are reading this, I am grateful to you, for holding this dream in your hands, for being part of making it a material reality.

Immense gratitude to the poets who read this collection with care and wrote the blurbs crowning the back cover. To Traci Brimhall, for writing openly, and with gorgeous rigor, about the experience of motherhood and then reading my poems with such deep empathy. To Linda Gregerson, for being an unforgettable workshop instructor at Bread Loaf while I was pregnant with my son, well before most of this book's poems existed, and then reading into their histories with a profound embrace of its complexities and ambiguities. To Ilya Kaminsky, my role model for writing in English, our adopted mother's tongue, while still reaching back to the music of Russian poets and our pasts in Ukraine, from where our families emigrated the same year, thank you for devouring my book with such fervor and being attentive to the crafting of its individual poems.

To Ellen Bass, not only for truly seeing the vision of this book and selecting it for publication, but for reading its poems with a care and attention I never could have imagined or hoped for. Our two-hour phone call about your suggested revisions will be one I keep looking back on and learning from for years and books to come.

Thank you to all the dedicated people at the Wick Poetry Center and Kent State University Press, for believing in this book and bringing it into the world: Christine Brooks, Richard Fugini, Jessica Jewell, Györgyi Mihályi-Jewell, Susan Wadsworth-Booth, and Mary D. Young. A special thanks to David Hassler, for taking the time to read even more of my poems and provide invaluable feedback on their place in the manuscript, and also for making the excited phone call that changed my life.

With great appreciation for the following institutions who have supported the making of this book throughout its various stages: The University of Maryland, The University of Oregon, The University of Pennsylvania, The Yiddish Book Center's Tent: Creative Writing Conference, The United States Holocaust Museum and Memorial (USHMM), The Auschwitz Jewish Center, The Hadassah–Brandeis Institute's Ruth G. Newman Research Award, and The Bread Loaf Writer's Conference.

To all the wonderful baristas at Ultimo Coffee on 22nd and Catherine—where most of this manuscript was composed—thank you for fueling my writing with the best extra hot lattes.

Gratitude to my many multidisciplinary mentors in the field of Holocaust studies, from fellow writers to researchers: Al Filreis, Annette Finley-Croswhite, Judith Greenberg, Elana Jankel, Courtney Sender, and Anika Walke.

My unending thanks to the creative writing teachers and mentors throughout my life: Ms. Finn, now Mrs. Sharyn Finn Bergman, who introduced me to expressing myself in English through poetry in the third grade; Donald Berger and Michael Collier, whose poetry workshops at the University of Maryland taught me how to tear my poems apart, so I could piece them back together stronger; and to Michael, for continuing to support my work for years after being your student. To my MFA professors at the University of Oregon: Geri Doran, for being the most attentive reader and thesis advisor, and always pushing my poems to discover their most brutal truths, you have been a guiding lyric voice; and Garrett Hongo, for teaching me what it means to listen to the music of the past and bring it into the present, for encouraging my obsession with telling and retelling that which refused to be told, and most of all, for reading an earlier draft of this book and suggesting I put the traumatic past in conversation with the sensual present of motherhood; without this advice, the arch of this book would not have emerged. To Anya Krugovoy Silver, taken from us too soon, I wish I could have told you that your poems, and your belief in mine, have changed my life, encouraging me to keep going when I'd lost hope because your magic was to always have faith. I will keep reading your words and writing with you and listening to your voice, of strength and history and motherhood. Thank you, eternally.

To my devoted advisors at the University of Pennsylvania, Kevin M. F. Platt and Paul Saint-Amour, thank you for supporting my blend of scholarship and creative writing, for believing in my ability to manage it all while mothering, and understanding that family always comes first. Kevin, you have opened my poetry even more to the Russian literary and cultural history from which it rises. Paul, you have taught me to listen even closer to language, and I know this strengthened my writing. You always reminded me to give myself credit for the efforts that might go unseen, thank you for seeing me so clearly, for helping me to see myself this way too. Thanks to the many other Penn faculty who have influenced me as a poet and scholar: David Eng, Kathryn Hellerstein, Jo Park, and Liliane Weissberg. And thanks to my doctoral peers, who helped me balance the poet and academic life, supporting my pursuit of both: Tim Chandler, Alison Howard, Pavel Khazanov, Alex Moshkin, Ariel Resnikoff, Iuliia Skubytska, and Orchid Tierney.

To the poets I am lucky enough to call friends, who have been there as readers throughout the writing and rewriting of this manuscript during the five years it took to become a book. Thank you for your eyes and ears, my UO MFA peers and the poets I've met at workshops since: Tina Mozelle Braziel, Chen Chen, Luke Hollis, Cate Lycurgus, Jenna Lynch, sam sax, and Carl Swart. My dear Sam Herschel Wein, thank you for your responses to frantic emails of draft poems, your honest feedback, and most of all, for your constant positivity and infectious spirit. Thank you to my poetry-soul-sister, Kelly Grace Thomas, for all of our poem and soul exchanges, for believing so fiercely in me and this book. Gratitude to Katie Condon and Flower Conroy, who graciously read earlier drafts of the manuscript in its entirety and helped it reach its final form. Thank you to my fellow Philly poet, Steven Kleinman, my partner in coffee-shop-writing crime, not only for providing essential line-edits, revision suggestions, and motivation to keep writing, but also for being there to listen to me complain about the long process of submission and rejection. Thank you, Ross White, for our Grinds where so many of these poems emerged or found their final forms, and for the inspiring way you champion emerging poets, the way you believe in our voices even when we stop believing in them ourselves. Thank you to my fellow Mama-poets who understand how motherhood seeps into not only the subject matter of our work, but the very craft of writing, Sara Rebeka Burnett, Maya Jewell Zeller, and Alexis Zimberg. Thank you all for encouraging me to keep writing and submitting in the face of any rejection, you've all helped make this book possible.

To my all my Fit4Mom Philly Mamas, but especially Kelsey Rose Clark, Anna Demetriou, Kim Martin Freidman, Sarah Mayland, Sara McDonald, Sara Strehle Meccia, and Sara Brohawn Rivas, thank you for your honest motherhood. It has helped motivate the writing of "Other women don't tell you" poems and the blog that followed.

To Stephanie Ruiz Dasbach, thank you for being the sister I never had and the Momma with whom I can share my worries and feelings of inadequacy at all hours, learning from the way you've dedicated yourself to raising four incredible children without losing sight of who you are.

To Gina Belopolskaya, my dearest best-friend-Mama, I am in awe of your strength, selflessness, and kindness. Thank you for all you've taught me about raising strong-willed boys while challenging the confines of our cultural upbringing, lessons that echo between the lines of these poems.

To Anna Belopolskaya, I am beyond grateful for your tireless work on designing a gorgeous cover that brought my vision to life in ways I couldn't have imagined, but even more grateful for the decades of best-friendship I've been lucky enough to share with you.

To my husband, the Papa-Honey who made me a Mama, my love, I could write you infinite words of gratitude, but language to express this would always fall short. This book exists because of your undying faith in me.

Because you refused to let me give up on poetry when my doubts would weigh heavier than my passion. Because you listen to every draft, immerse yourself in the world of my poems, and remind me that others should get to hear them. Because you support and understand the time away from family writing requires, taking care of our son whenever I have a reading or need to escape into my words, and you do so with nothing but compassion, never letting me feel guilty for my work. Thank you for making me feel loved and appreciated every day, for being the most devoted father, and for becoming a doting son and grandson to my Mamachka and Babushka.

To my Mamachka and Babushka and Pra-Babushka, the mothers I come from who inspired this book, thank you and Papa and Dedushka, for being brave enough to leave your homeland, to give up everything, so I could grow up in a place where I am free to express myself through writing. My Pra-Babuhska, great-grandmother Vera, your legacy lingers in every poem. Thank you for teaching me history and struggle, strength and resilience. Thank you for your love, which I remember each time I say my son's name. My Babushka, grandmother Rita, you are the spine of this book, the one who binds these poems and our family. Thank you for your wisdom and the stories you've shared so I could imagine a past I never knew. I appreciate how you read my poems in a language that will always remain foreign to you, and without understanding every word, thank you for feeling the emotions I try to convey. To my Mamachka, Svetlana, thank you for raising me on poetry and art and music, for always believing in the power of verse and showing me what it can do. Thank you for teaching me what it means to be a Mama and for supporting my journey of motherhood even when it diverged with yours. Everything I have ever accomplished, or could hope to in the future, is because of who you raised me to be, because of how special you have made me feel every day of my life. When I see myself through your eyes, anything seems possible, like this very book. Thank you, my three pillars of motherhood, Vera, Rita, and Svetlana. Thank you for being the most committed Mamas who always put their children first. I am honored to follow in your footsteps as I balance art and family, striving to be a fraction of the mother you have all been, but comforted by the knowledge that my son is lucky enough to know and be loved by his Babushka and Pra-Babushka.

And to my son, Valen, my Val'ushka, my love who named me Mama, this book is because of you, it is for you. Its poems are the first of what I know will be many attempts to show you where we come. May our history teach you to love in the face of hate, create in the face of destruction, and hope—always hope—in the face of everything else.

NOTES

"Against Naming"
Oświęcim is the Polish town renamed Auschwitz by the Germans when they invaded and turned farmland into the concentration camp, Auschwitz I, and then the death camp, Auschwitz II-Birkenau. The "big book of names" refers to the document/memorial/installation, which takes up an entire room of Block 27 within the Auschwitz-Birkenau Memorial and Museum and lists all the known names of Holocaust victims.

"Learning Yiddish"
I. My great-grandmother's Yiddish exclamation, "Gotteniu tayer. Gotteniu vey zmir" translates to "Dear God. God woe is me."
V. "Pryaniki" are a traditional spiced honey cookies common across Russia, Ukraine, and Belarus.
VI. "и она его любила" is Russian meaning "and she loved him." "Kindzmarauli" is type of Georgian dessert wine. "но она его любила" is Russian meaning "even though she loved him."
VIII. "Babi Yar," or "Бабий Яр" in Russian, which literally translates to "an old woman's ravine," is a mass grave in Ukraine's capital city, Kiev, where in the span of two days, from September 29th through the 30th, 1941, more than 33,000 Jews are estimated to have been shot by Nazis and their local Ukrainian collaborators. This is where my family believes my great-grandfather was likely murdered, but his name remains unfound. "Nomen" is the Yiddish word for "name."

"Why I Never Wore My Mother's Pearls"
"Zhem-choog," or "жемчуг" in Russian, is the word for pearls.

"The Book of Mothers"
"Chernozem," or "Чернозём" in Russian, comes from "chorny" meaning "black" and "zemlya" meaning earth. It refers to the fertile black soil that stretches across the Eurasian steppe.

"While everything falls apart, imagine how you'll teach your son about guns"
This poem refers to a song from the famous Soviet cartoon about the Bremen Musicians, "Бременские музыканты." The song is performed by the

musicians when they are dressed up as the bad-guy bandits, and the ono-matopoetic words "bang, bang" are "peef, paf," or "пиф-паф" in Russian.

"Names of *Svet*"
"Svet," or "Свет," is the Russian word for light.

"Diagnosis: Takotsubo"
Takotsubo cardiomyopathy is the clinical term for the colloquial broken heart syndrome. It is a sudden, temporary weakening of the muscular portion of the heart, which can be fatal—what we would call dying of a broken heart. "Takotsubo" is the Japanese word for "octopus trap" because the left ventricle of the heart resembles its shape when the muscle weakens.

"the mourning customs of elephants"
The shot referred to in the poem is RhoGAM, a shot used for the last fifty years for women with an Rh-negative blood type to prevent infertility in a second pregnancy, which was common prior to this medical intervention.

there is no name for this.
"Sharik," or "шарик," is the Russian word for balloon.

"bab'e lyeto / бабье лето"
Literally translates to "old woman's summer." The word "baba" means old woman and is also used as the shortened form of "Babushka," meaning "grandmother."

"Camp means field"
"Lagrima" is the word for teardrop in Spanish. "Lager" is the shortened form of the German, "konzentrationslager," meaning "concentration camp." Similar to the word "camp" in English, in Russian the word "lager'" or "лагерь" can refer to both summer camps and a concentration camps, depending on the context. "Lagend" refers to a wreckage on a seabed that is attached to a buoy so that it can be recovered.

"Inheritance"
"Zhid," or "жид," is a derogatory, anti-Semitic slur in the Russian language, similar to the word "kike." It comes from the word for Jew in many Slavic languages like Ukrainian.

Printed in the United States
by Baker & Taylor Publisher Services